BRIGHT

TO KILL A MOCKINGBIRD BY HARPER LEE

Intelligent Education

Nashville, Tennessee

BRIGHT NOTES: To Kill a Mockingbird
www.BrightNotes.com

No part of this publication may be used or reproduced in any manner whatsoever without written permission, except in the case of brief quotations in critical articles and reviews. For permissions, contact Influence Publishers http://www.influencepublishers.com.

ISBN: 978-1-645421-82-5 (Paperback)
ISBN: 978-1-645421-83-2 (eBook)

Published in accordance with the U.S. Copyright Office Orphan Works and Mass Digitization report of the register of copyrights, June 2015.

Originally published by Monarch Press.
Donald F. Roden; Randall Blum; Susan O'Leary; W. John Campbell, 1965
2019 Edition published by Influence Publishers.

Interior design by Lapiz Digital Services. Cover Design by Thinkpen Designs.

Printed in the United States of America.

Library of Congress Cataloging-in-Publication Data forthcoming.
Names: Intelligent Education
Title: BRIGHT NOTES: To Kill a Mockingbird
Subject: STU004000 STUDY AIDS / Book Notes

CONTENTS

1) Introduction to Harper Lee — 1

2) Textual Analysis
    Part I — 7
    Part II — 24

3) Character Analyses — 47

4) Commentary — 56

5) Critical Commentary — 65

6) Essay Questions and Answers — 69

7) Bibliography — 74

INTRODUCTION TO HARPER LEE

EARLY LIFE

Born in Monroeville, Alabama, on April 28, 1926, Nelle Harper Lee is the youngest of three children of Amassa Coleman Lee and Francis Lee. Before his death, Miss Lee's father and her older sister, Alice, practiced law together in Monroeville. When one considers the **theme** of honor that runs throughout Miss Lee's novel, it is perhaps significant to note that her family is related to Confederate General Robert E. Lee, a man especially noted for his devotion to that virtue.

Miss Lee received her early education in the Monroeville public schools. Following this, she entered the University of Alabama to study law. She left there to spend a year in England as an exchange student. Returning to the university, she continued her studies, but left in 1950 without having completed the requirements for her law degree. She moved to New York and worked as an airline reservation clerk.

CHARACTER

It is said that Miss Lee personally resembles the tomboy she describes in the character of Scout. Her dark straight hair is worn cut in a short style. Her main interests, she says, are "collecting the memoirs of nineteenth century clergymen, golf, crime, and music." She is a Whig in political thought and believes in "Catholic emancipation and the repeal of the corn laws."

SOURCES OF *TO KILL A MOCKINGBIRD*

Among the sources for Miss Lee's novel are the following:

1. National events: This novel focuses on the role of the Negro in Southern life, a life with which Miss Lee has been intimately associated. Although it does not deal with civil rights as such - for example, the right to vote - it is greatly concerned with the problem of human dignity - dignity based on individual merit, not racial origin. The bigotry of the characters in this novel greatly resembles that of the people in the South today, where the fictional Maycomb County is located.

2. Specific Persons: Atticus Finch is the principal character in this novel. He bears a close resemblance to Harper Lee's father, whose middle name was Finch. In addition to both being lawyers, they are similar in character and personality - humble, intelligent and hard-working.

3. Personal Experience: Boo Radley's house has an aura of fantasy, superstition, and curiosity for the Finch children. There was a similar house in Harper Lee's childhood. Furthermore, Miss Lee grew up amid the Negro prejudice and violence in Alabama. In addition, she studied law and visited her father's law offices as a child, just as Scout visits Atticus' office and briefly considers a career as a lawyer.

WRITING CAREER

Harper Lee began to develop an interest in writing at the age of seven. Her law studies proved to be good training for a writing career: they promote logical thinking, and legal cases are an excellent source of story ideas. After she came to New York, she approached a literary agent with a manuscript of two essays and three short stories. Miss Lee followed his suggestion that she expand one of the stories into a novel. This eventually became *To Kill A Mockingbird*.

After the success of her first novel, Miss Lee returned to Monroeville to begin work on a second one. She learned quickly that privacy was not one of the prizes of a best-selling novelist. "These southern people are southern people," she said, "and if they know you are working at home, they think nothing of walking in for coffee." Miss Lee also has said that her second novel will be about the South, for she is convinced that her section of the country is "the refuge of genuine eccentrics."

Miss Lee thinks of herself as a journeyman writer, and of writing as the most difficult work in the world. Her workday begins at noon and continues until early evening. At the end of this time, she may have completed a page or two. Before rewriting, she always allows some time to elapse, for a fresh viewpoint on what she has done.

Besides her prize-winning novel, Miss Lee has had several essays published. For example, "Christmas to Me" appeared in the December, 1961, issue of McCalls, and "Love - In other Words" appeared in the April 15, 1961, edition of *Vogue*. These essays display the same easy, sympathetic style of her novel.

BRIGHT NOTES STUDY GUIDE

SUCCESS OF *TO KILL A MOCKINGBIRD*

The success of Harper Lee's novel, *To Kill A Mockingbird*, can be assessed from its appearance on the bestseller lists for a period of over eighty weeks. Also the book was chosen as a Literary Guild selection; a Book-of-the-Month book; and a Reader's Digest Condensed Book. It was also published in paperback by Popular Library. In April, 1961, Miss Lee was awarded the Alabama Library Association Award. In May, 1961, she was the first woman since 1942 to win the $500.00 Pulitzer Prize for fiction. In addition to its acclaim in the United States, *To Kill A Mockingbird* has received awards in foreign countries. For example, in Britain it was selected British Book Society Top Book of the Year. It remained on the British book lists as a top seller for many months. Besides this, it has been translated into several foreign languages. This is an unusual amount of honor to be conferred on any novel; that an author's first work should receive such recognition is truly extraordinary.

BACKGROUND OF THE NOVEL

Early South

In order to appreciate *To Kill A Mockingbird* fully, the reader should be familiar with some of the background of its setting. The South in the colonial times grew into an area with large cotton plantations and small cities. Because of the necessity for cheap labor to pick and seed the cotton, Negro slavery took a stronghold there. At the outbreak of the American Revolution, there were over 500,000 slaves in this country, with by far the greatest number in the South. As time passed, plantation owners formed a landed aristocracy. The Negroes, though slaves, gained a measure of economic security. On the perimeter of this were the poorer white farmers who either owned small pieces of land or worked as sharecroppers.

Civil War

With the invention of machines like the cotton gin, that could do the work of many men, the need for slaves began to decrease. The profitability of slavery also decreased, and plantation owners often treated Negroes with less kindness. There were two extremes. A few Southerners gave their slaves freedom, while others totally disregarded them. The Civil War brought slavery to an end, but created other, worse problems. The carpetbaggers who streamed into the South for political and economic gain aggravated the wounds which the war had opened. The Negro was caught in the middle. On the one hand, the Northerners claimed to be working for his benefit, but were really doing little. On the other, the Southerners began to take out their bitterness for the Yankees on the Negroes. The colored man represented two things to the Southerner. First, he was a slave who was now forcibly being given equal rights with his former master. Second, he was the symbol of defeat, and a reminder of what the North had done to the South. Therefore, he became an outcast, a scapegoat to be subjugated and mistreated.

Post Civil War

As time passed and new methods for farming and cotton production were developed, many people in Southern rural areas became extremely poor. Some moved to the city; others stayed on the land to try to get whatever was possible out of it. Then, in 1929, the Great Depression hit the United States. The farmers seemed to suffer most because they depended entirely upon their land for a living. Their crops rotted, and they had little or no money for seed. But, in 1932, a new era was ushered into American political and economic life. With Franklin Roosevelt, the federal government began to take an active interest in the workingman. Laws regulating farm production, labor unions, and social security became a part of the American way of life. A new social consciousness was arousing many people in the nation.

Novel In Its Setting

To Kill A Mockingbird is set against this background of 1930 Southern life. The Finches are a family who once had a large, successful plantation. Their ancestors had been aristocratic ladies and gentlemen of the South. Now they have been reduced to gentile poverty. They are better off by far than the Cunninghams, for example, who have nothing but their land. Atticus Finch has his law career, and Alexandra is still able to make a living at Finch's Landing. Actually, the extremes of poverty are illustrated in the Ewells and the Negroes. The Ewells are poor, but they don't want to do anything about it. The Negroes are poor because nobody will let them do anything about it. The Ewells won't work even when they can. The Negroes will work, but the only jobs available to them are the menial, low-paying ones.

TO KILL A MOCKINGBIRD

TEXTUAL ANALYSIS

PART I

CHAPTER 1

Scout (Jean Louise) Finch narrates the story, beginning with a brief family history. Simon Finch, a fur-trapping apothecary journeyed from England to Alabama, establishing the family which made its living from cotton on Simon's homestead, Finch's Landing. The Civil War left the family only its land, which was the source of family incomes until the twentieth century when Atticus Finch (Scout's father) and his brother Jack left the land for careers in law and medicine. Atticus settled in Maycomb, the county seat of Maycomb County, with a reasonably successful law practice about twenty miles from Finch's Landing, where his sister Alexandra still lived.

Scout describes Maycomb as a lethargic, hot, colorless, narrow-minded town where she lives with her father, brother Jem (four years older) and the family cook, Calpurnia. Scout's mother had died when she was two.

When she was five, Scout and Jem found a new friend, Dill Harris ("Goin' on seven"), next door in Miss Rachel Haverford's collard patch. Dill was Miss Rachel's nephew from Meridian, Mississippi, who spent summers in Maycomb.

In the summertime, Jem, Scout and Dill usually played within the boundaries of Mrs. Henry Dubose's house (two doors north) and the Radley place (three doors south). The Radley place fascinated the children, because it was a popular subject of gossip and superstition in Maycomb. Arthur Radley had gotten into trouble with the law when he was a boy. Instead of being sent to the state industrial school, his father took custody of him within their house. He was not seen again for fifteen years. Many legends grew up about the Radley house and about what went on inside. Miss Stephanie Crawford, a neighborhood gossip, added fuel to the fire - a fire which included stories of crime, mutilation, curses and insanity.

Dill was fascinated by these stories, and gave Scout and Jem the idea of making Boo Radley come out of seclusion. When Dill, always eager for some new adventure, dared Jem to run up to the house and touch it, Jem thought things over for a few days. Finally, filled with fear, he accepted the dare. He ran up, touched the house, and ran back. As the three children stared at the old house, they thought they saw an inside shutter move.

Comment

Many **themes** and plot-themes emerge in Chapter 1. Great emphasis is placed on the world of Scout, Jem, and Dill - a small world bounded by a few houses and composed of only a few people. From the limited knowledge of this small childish world at the novel's opening, Jem and Scout broaden with the passing of years and events. By the time the novel reaches its conclusion, they will have learned much more about human nature. Also, Miss Lee emphasizes the Radley family. They are the focal point for the development of numerous themes to come. For example, when old Mr. Radley died, Calpurnia did something she had never been known to do before. She spoke evil about a white man when she said, "There goes the meanest man ever God blew breath into." Finally, there are the **themes** relating to family and the Maycomb setting. They increase in importance from chapter to chapter.

Notes

amble - to walk leisurely

nebulous - not clear

predilection - preference

repertoire - the collection of plays, songs, etc., with which a performer is familiar

transition - a change

vapid - not interesting

CHAPTERS 2 AND 3

Scout At School

Dill returned to Mississippi at the end of the summer. Although she was looking forward to school more than anything in her life, Scout's first day at school was a disappointment. When Miss

Caroline tried to teach reading, Scout was bored. Much to Miss Caroline's dismay, Scout was already accomplished at reading and writing. She told Scout to tell her father not to teach her anything more, because it would interfere with her reading. Later, at lunchtime, Walter Cunningham had no food with him. When the teacher tried to give him a quarter, the boy would not take it. Scout made the mistake of trying to explain the reason to Miss Caroline. The Cunninghams were poor country folks who had been hit hard by the Depression and were too proud to accept charity. For her trouble, Scout got her fingers cracked. Thinking that Walter Cunningham was the cause of her difficulty, Scout tried to beat him up. Jem would not let her. Instead, he invited the boy to lunch at their house.

That afternoon, Miss Caroline saw a cootie crawl out of Burris Ewell's hair. She was shocked by this and told the boy to go home and wash his hair. The boy really did not care, however, and became abusive, since he was in school only because the truant officer had made him come. He did not plan to return. That night Scout had a talk with her father. She said she hoped that Atticus would allow her to stay home from school like Burris Ewell. However, he explained to her that the Ewells were a different kind of people. They did not care about learning and had been a disgrace to Maycomb for generations. Then Atticus made a bargain with his daughter. He told Scout that he would continue to read to her every night provided she would go back to school and promise not to tell her teacher about it.

Comment These two chapters can be considered together for they contain the story of Scout's first experience away from her narrow world at home. The reader must remember that although she was bright for her age, Scout was only six. Whatever she had learned thus far, she had learned at

home from her father, her brother, Calpurnia, and a few neighbors. Therefore, she had much to learn from and about the rest of the world. For example, Scout was a town girl and not a farm girl like many of the other children in the class. Miss Caroline, the teacher, was not from Maycomb, and could not be expected to know or to understand the peculiarities of the people of Maycomb. The little girl could not comprehend why Miss Caroline did not have a better understanding. With her limited experience, Scout thought that people were alike everywhere. Therefore, she thought that her teacher should automatically know that the Cunninghams were poor. Also she thought that her teacher should understand that the Cunninghams, and other people of Maycomb, were too proud to accept anything that they could not pay back. But Maycomb was farm country, and farmers were a "set breed of men," prizing independence more than a full stomach. Miss Caroline was from the city; Scout learned that city people were different.

Miss Caroline: Note, however, that Miss Caroline seemed to have learned something that first day at school too. In the morning, she became disturbed when Scout tried to tell her about Walter Cunningham. In the afternoon she was quite willing to listen to one of the older children when he explained to her about Burris Ewell. Thus the reader will find this entire novel is a series of experiences in which one character will gain new insights from his association with the others.

New Names: There are two important new names introduced in these chapters - Walter Cunningham and Burris Ewell. Both are from the poor, rural section of the county. However, the reader should notice the difference in their characters. Walter is proud and independent; he won't accept charity. He apologizes for still being in the first grade. At lunch Atticus speaks to him about farming as though he were a grown man. On the other hand, Burris Ewell is surly. He dares Miss Caroline to make him do anything. Here, therefore, the author presents the reader with the first series of character contrasts. These will be important to the reader throughout the entire novel, especially if he expects to be able to understand fully the **theme** of the story.

Notes

transaction - business deal

cunning - attractive in a skillful way

illicitly - unlawfully

vexations - annoyances

mortification - humiliation

iniquities - sins

fractious - unruly, irritable

CHAPTERS 4, 5 AND 6

Radley's Oak Tree

Because Scout was in the first grade, she got out of school thirty minutes earlier than her brother. This meant a walk home alone past the dreaded Radley house. Usually she would run by it. There were two giant oaks on the Radley property. One day as Scout was running past, she noticed something shiny in a knothole of one of the trees. Examining it, she found two pieces of chewing gum. When she decided they were all right to eat, she put them into her mouth. When Jem came home, he made her spit out the gum. Anything found on the Radley place might be poison. On the last day of school the children found a box with two pennies in it. They did not know what to make of the situation, but they decided to keep the pennies.

Dill Returns

Two days later Dill arrived. As usual he was full of wild stories and anxious to play games of make-believe. The group decided to play a game modeled on the life of Boo Radley. One of the stories about him was that he had stabbed his father with a pair of scissors, so the children began to act this out every day. They continued until Atticus caught them and took away the scissors.

While the two boys played a scissorless version of their Boo Radley game, Scout became friendly with Miss Maudie Atkinson, a benevolent neighbor who had grown up with Atticus' brother Jack. The two of them would sit on Miss Maudie's porch and talk. One day they had a talk about Boo Radley and Miss Maudie tried to explain the mystery of the Radley family. Recalling that Arthur had been nice to her as a boy, she called the Radley house a sad place. She denied the rumors about Boo as "three-fourth colored folks and one-fourth Stephanie Crawford." The next morning Jem and Dill decided they would try to drop a note into the Radley house by using a fishing pole. While they were doing this, Atticus came by and once more warned them about bothering the Radleys.

On the last night before Dill had to return home to Mississippi, the boys hatched a plot. They decided to sneak through the back of the Radley property and take a peek through one of the windows. While doing this, they saw the shadow of a man pass by. As they ran toward the back fence, a shotgun blast went off. The three of them hurried even more and managed to escape. However, when they got home, Jem realized that he had lost his pants. He had had to squirm out of them while crawling under the Radley fence. Thus he found himself faced with another problem. That night, after everyone had gone to bed, he went back after his pants. Luckily, they were still there.

Comment

These chapters reveal the children's reaction to the Radley place, and to the Radleys themselves. It is a typically childish viewpoint. For example, Scout could not eat the gum because anything found on the Radley place might be poison. Also in these chapters there is childish imitation. The life which the Radleys led was very unusual. The family remained almost constantly in the house. The children, with a natural inclination to imitate the unusual in the adult world, wanted to play the Radley game. The Radley game was their Maycomb substitute for playing cowboys and Indians. With a typical childlike love of adventure and a curiosity to discover the unknown, Scout, Jem and Dill longed to discover the answer to the Radley mystery. They could not understand it as Atticus or Miss Maudie did. They had to try to find out for themselves what went on inside the secretive home. Thus the incident of the note on the end of the fishing pole and the night visit. Notice, however, that although the children are curious, they are not foolishly brave. For example, they have the length of the fishing pole between them and the house. Also they chose the darkness of night to sneak up to the window.

Notes

auspicious - successful, favorable

ethical - moral

reluctantly - unwillingly

benevolence - kindness

quibbling - petty arguing

CHAPTER 7

School started again. "The second grade was as bad as the first, only worse." One afternoon, Jem told Scout that when he returned to get his pants, they were hanging over the fence. Someone had mended the tear - "Not like a lady sewed 'em, ... All crooked." After this, the children began to find more things in the tree. First a ball of twine; then two soap dolls; and finally an old watch. They decided they should write a thank-you note to whoever was giving them these things. However, when they went to put the note into the knothole, Jem and Scout found that it had been filled in with cement. Nathan Radley, Boo's brother, said he had done this because the tree was dying and this was the way to save it. Atticus home from work and told Jem, "That tree's as healthy as you are." Scout noticed that Jem had been crying when he came in that night.

Comment

In this chapter the children begin to stop taking things for granted. They try to figure out how the articles in the tree got there. When they conclude that it is probably Boo Radley who is putting them there, they do the logical thing. They write a note which they intend to put into the tree. There is a difference, however, in the way in which each one reacts to the cement. Scout is still very young. She knows that Nathan Radley is being mean, but it does not affect her personally. On the other hand, the older Jem is more sensitive and feels things more deeply. He cries not for himself but for Boo Radley. He cannot comprehend how one man can be deliberately cruel to another. In his childlike way, Jem realizes that Boo Radley must have enjoyed putting those articles into the tree for them. Jem also realizes that the man was very considerate to sew his pants. Because of his youth, he does not know how to fight adult cruelty. Thus he cries.

CHAPTER 8

Usually Maycomb had hot summers and mild winters. When snow fell one night, Scout thought it was the end of the world. She had never seen it before. Because of this unexpected cold weather, everyone had fires going at home. During the night, Miss Maudie's house caught fire. Since all the houses were old wooden ones, everyone had to go out into the cold night. While Scout was watching the firemen at work, someone slipped a blanket around her shoulders. Later, first Jem and then Atticus realize that Boo Radley must have done this. Jem is afraid to return the blanket; he is afraid of what Nathan may do to Boo. Atticus agrees that they should keep the blanket and the incident to themselves.

Comment

Kindness is a prominent **theme** in this chapter. There is the unexpected kindness of Boo Radley. An air of mystery pervades the blanket incident because no one realizes at the time that the action is being taken. The effect on Scout is typical. She is all right until it dawns on her what has happened. Then she is sick with fright at the thought that Boo Radley stood right behind her and touched her. On the other hand, Jem reacts differently again. His first concern is Boo. In a babbling attempt to defend him, Jem blurts out the story of his pants to Atticus. His compassion is genuine. He is afraid of what Nathan may do to Boo. As soon as his fear for Boo is relieved, however, he relaxes and makes a joke at Scout's expense - he re-enacts the scene for her benefit, frightening her terribly.

Miss Maudie

Courage is also an important **theme**, embodied in Miss Maudie's character. The day after her house burned down, she did not wallow in self-pity. She laughed and said that she was glad that the whole thing had happened. Now she would be able to build a smaller house, take in roomers, and have more room for the plants which she loved so dearly. The children were perplexed by her unexpected good humor, but they admired her good-natured bravery in the face of personal tragedy.

Notes

unfathomable - not understandable

aberration - a departure from what is right or correct

perpetrate - to do or perform something

perplexity - confusion

BRIGHT NOTES STUDY GUIDE

CHAPTER 9

Chapter 9 introduces the reader to the main action of the story - Atticus Finch's defense of the Negro Tom Robinson. "Maycomb's usual disease," as Atticus calls it, begins to show itself. The narrow-minded bigotry of the townspeople and of the Finch family is hard for Scout to cope with. First there was Cecil Jacobs who announced in the schoolyard that Scout's daddy defended "niggers." Scout denied it, but ran home to get an explanation. Atticus told her that he was going to defend Tom Robinson, a member of Calpurnia's church. He explains that the case is very important to him personally, and requests that Jem and Scout try to ignore the talk they will hear around town. Next day, Scout is ready to fight Cecil Jacobs again, but remembers Atticus' request and walks away from a fight for the first time in her life.

Sometime later they left for Finch's Landing for the customary family Christmas celebration with Uncle Jack, Aunt Alexandra and cousin Francis. Francis taunts Scout by calling Atticus a "nigger-lover," saying that "he's ruinin' the family." Scout flies to her father's defense with fists and "bathroom invective," but gets a spanking from Uncle Jack. Later he apologizes when he hears her side of the story, and promises not to tell Atticus what Scout and Francis really fought about.

Comment

This chapter is very important if the reader is going to understand the full meaning of this novel. Atticus has been appointed to defend a Negro. Scout is ridiculed by one of her schoolmates because of this. Here is shown the attitude of the townspeople toward the Negroes. Then on Christmas Scout hears the same talk from her cousin Francis. This shows the attitude of the Finch family itself about the problem. Both Cecil Jacobs and Francis are, of course, echoing what they have heard the adults say on the subject. Obviously, to both family and townspeople it seems that Atticus Finch is making a mistake. How does Scout act about this matter: She wants to fight with her fists. But she soon learns that this is not the way to combat a dispute over ideas. Uncle Jack spanks her, but in her mind he has been unfair. Uncle Jack had not listened to her side of the story. When she can tell him about it in the quiet of her room, he says that he is sorry.

SCOUT AND THE ADULTS

What then is the picture of the world in the mind of this child, and how does it foreshadow the future events of the story? At first Scout fights with her fists because she does not know how to fight any other way. Then she sees adult injustice applied to her by Uncle Jack, someone whom she loves. She begins to realize that lack of knowledge and lack of forethought often lead people to do things that they might not otherwise do. Later, when Scout sees the injustice performed by the people against the Negro Tom Robinson, she is going to be able to have just a little bit better understanding of the reasons for it.

Notes

analogous - similar

provocation - something or someone who causes anger in another

romp - generally to play, but here to scold or punish

scurry - to run in a hurried manner

CHAPTER 10

The first nine chapters give us a picture of Atticus Finch as a kind and understanding man. He is also an upright man who is trying to raise his children properly. In this chapter we get a clearer picture of him. First we see him through the eyes of his children. To them he is old and feeble because he can't play football. Then an event occurs to change this picture. A mad dog comes down the street. It is Atticus who is called upon to do the shooting. His children see him now as a brave man. Scout wants to brag about this to all her friends, but Jem tells her not to.

Comment

To the reader this chapter might seem out of place. It appears to be an unrelated incident. However, it serves to help prepare the reader for what is to follow. In a sense, it sums up the character of Atticus Finch. Thus far we have seen him as a very quiet and serious person. Now the author shows another side of his character. He is brave but in a different way. He does the day-to-day actions so well that when he is called upon to do an extraordinary action, its performance comes naturally to him.

Scout Vs. Jem

Again we see a contrast in the attitude of the two children. The younger Scout still cannot understand why things should or should not be done. For example, she cannot understand why Atticus never told his children about his ability to shoot. On the other hand, Jem, the older child, is beginning to have a sense of values. He realizes that being a man, and more importantly, a gentleman, is not just in acting and talking. It is knowing when to act and when to talk. In childlike simplicity he says, "Atticus is a gentleman, just like me." More than ever he wants to be like his father.

Notes

contemporaries - those living at the same time

tartly - sourly

mausoleum - tomb

articulate - able to speak

CHAPTER 11

Mrs. Henry Lafayette Dubose, an old lady who lived near the Finch house, made a point of being cantankerous and scolded Jem and Scout every time she saw them. Sometimes she would scold them for something they did; sometimes for the way they were dressed. The children, of course, hated her, but there was nothing they could do about it. One day she made some remarks about Atticus, calling him a "nigger-lover." On the way home that day, Jem took the baton which he had bought for his sister and used it to wreck all of Mrs. Dubose's camellias. When Atticus learned of this, he made Jem apologize. Jem had to read to Mrs. Dubose every day for a month. During this time she had repeated fits which frightened Scout. Soon after, Mrs. Dubose died. Atticus then explained to the children that she had been a morphine addict. When she found out that she did not have long to live, she determined to break the habit. The purpose of Jem's reading was to distract her attention while she was having her fits. By the time of her death, she had won her battle.

Comment

At the close of this chapter, Atticus refers to Mrs. Dubose as the bravest person he ever knew. This statement is difficult to understand, especially since it comes from a man whom she had openly abused. But Jem learns that sometimes people say and do things because they cannot help themselves. For example, Mrs. Dubose was a sick old lady. She took out her suffering on Scout and Jem. Yet fundamentally she was a courageous person. Atticus admired her strength of will and determination to die "beholden to nothing and nobody." This was adult bravery. Atticus wanted the children to understand that courage is more than "a man with a gun in his hand." The camellia which she sent to Jem was a symbol of strength. Jem had tried to destroy the shrubs, but they grew back because they were strong. Mrs. Dubose had almost been destroyed by morphine, but she conquered it finally. She was as strong as her camellias.

Adult Bravery

Chapter 11 brings Part I of this novel to a close. The children have seen three examples of adult bravery. First there was Miss Maudie who faced the difficulty of rebuilding her house after the fire. Then there was Atticus who never bragged about his ability to shoot. But when he was needed, he was unafraid to face the mad dog. Finally there was Mrs. Dubois who faced bravely the prospect of a painful death. Now Jem and Scout must come face to face with the greatest test of their young lives - the trial of Tom Robinson.

Notes

encounters - meetings

interrogation - questioning

umbrage - offense

oppressive - burdensome

interdict - an order that forbids certain actions

undulate - to move in a wavy motion

propensity - natural tendency

escapade - a reckless adventure

TO KILL A MOCKINGBIRD

TEXTUAL ANALYSIS

PART II

CHAPTER 12

This chapter introduces the reader to the second part of the novel. Atticus was away at the state capital, so Calpurnia asked the children if they wanted to go to church with her. Scout and Jem thus enter into the world of the Negro. There are many things which are strange to them. The Negroes, for example, do not sing from hymn books. Also Reverend Sykes is quite open - about the way he addresses his parishioners, even calling out the names of certain people who had done wrong. The collection that Sunday was for Helen Robinson, Tom's wife. Because Scout did not understand why she did not go to work, Reverend Sykes explained that no white person wanted to hire Tom Robinson's wife. Later, when Calpurnia and the children arrived home, they found Aunt Alexandra on the front porch waiting for them.

Comment

There are many interesting little points in this chapter which the reader should not pass over if he is going to appreciate its value to the story. First, there is the greater distance which is developing between the older Jem and the Little sister. He understands more easily and tries to be more serious than she. Furthermore, he is beginning to adopt a superior attitude where she is concerned. Secondly, there is the comment that Calpurnia makes to Lulu. This woman resented Jem and Scout coming to the Negro church. Calpurnia told her that it was the same God. Thirdly, when Reverend Sykes asked for more money for Helen, Jem insisted to Calpurnia that he and Scout use their own rather than what she wanted to give them. This shows his desire to be like the adults. Fourthly, there is the attitude of Calpurnia about the way she acts. She wants to be educated and to speak like the white folks; and yet with her own people, she acts and speaks as they do. All of these facts put Jem and Scout right into the middle of the Tom Robinson plot. Jem is trying to be mature, but Scout still does not understand many things. Both children are amazed by what they see in the Negro Church. They are also surprised by Calpurnia's actions. Scout cannot understand why the Negro woman would hide her knowledge when she was among her own people. But Calpurnia had her reasons, and they were good ones.

Calpurnia Vs. Lulu

In this chapter the reader might make a contrast between Calpurnia and Lulu. Calpurnia seemed to realize that if she were to be accepted by the white people, she would have to improve herself. Thus she had learned to read, and she had also taught her son Zeebo. On the other hand, not only did Lulu not want to be accepted by the white people, but she did not want to accept them when they came to her. The result was that Calpurnia did find a place where she was welcome. This is not to say that she was accepted into white society in general. However, she had become an important part of a white family which was willing to accept her for what she was personally. In fact, Atticus Finch looked upon Calpurnia not as a servant, but as a very necessary and much-loved member of his family.

Notes

appalling - frightening

bode - forecast

habiliments - articles of clothing

qualms - misgivings

enamored - ready for warfare

uncompromising - inflexible

CHAPTER 13

Aunt Alexandra came to spend the summer with her brother's family. Jem and Scout weren't very happy about this arrangement, Atticus knew that he would need all the help he could get during the trial of Tom Robinson. Aunt Alexandra made herself right at home, determined to have a "feminine influence" on Scout. Scout resigned herself to a long summer. Aunt Alexandra tries to tell the children about their family background and how proud they should be of it. Atticus at first told Jem and Scout that they should listen to her. However, he realized afterwards that her "preoccupation with heredity" and "gentle breeding" stemmed from a false sense of values. He told the children to forget it.

Comment

This chapter introduces the **theme** of the importance of family background and the caste system in Maycomb. Aunt Alexandra is impressed by a good name. To her this means a family who can trace its ancestry, and who has lived on the same land for a long period of time. Of course, she regards the Finch family and their estate, Finch's Landing, as inviolate proof of their moral and social worth. She would carefully conceal any black marks on the family name. For example, she is shocked to discover that the children know the story of their Cousin Joshua, who had been in jail for having tried to shoot another man. In contrast to his sister, Atticus gave little thought to family breeding. He was more interested in the personal value of an individual. He never told Jem and Scout much about the family background because he did not think it important enough to discuss. He did the best he could to give them a genuine sense of values and behavior.

Notes

formidable - causing fear

prerogative - privilege

tranquility - peacefulness

BRIGHT NOTES STUDY GUIDE

CHAPTER 14

A few days later Aunt Alexandra overheard Scout ask Atticus about going to visit at Calpurnia's house. Upset by this request, Alexandra urges her brother to fire the Negro cook, but he won't do it. Calpurnia has been a faithful member of the family too long. After the quarrel Jem tells Scout that she should avoid upsetting Atticus, because he's got a great deal to worry about with the trial. Scout thinks that Atticus wouldn't worry about anything. That night the children discovered Dill under Scout's bed. He had run away from home and he related a fictional tale of his neglect by his new father. He wasn't happy and wanted to be with his friends. Jem's act of treason in telling Atticus about Dill is forgiven when Atticus gets permission for Dill to stay.

Comment

This chapter re-emphasizes Aunt Alexandra's feelings about Negroes. She does not want her family associated with them in any way. Alexandra's main concern was the preservation of a good family name in order to keep one's place in society. When her two brothers left Finch's Landing, she stayed on to take care of the place. But her life was far from happy, for she had made an unfortunate marriage. Her husband was more interested in fishing than in anything else. Now she sees the family name in danger of being completely ruined by the Tom Robinson affair and by Calpurnia's influence.

Dill Vs. Alexandra

Dill provides a contrast to Aunt Alexandra. Where she puts faith in a family name, at the expense of truth and personal happiness,

Dill ran away from home to find happiness. The re-marriage of his mother should have given him security. Instead it gave him a greater feeling of not being wanted. In other words, mere home and family name were not enough. Dill had courage to seek happiness, instead of resigning to a false value system.

| Notes

ponder - think

rankling - festering

resilient - springy, like a spring

| CHAPTER 15

One night some men from town came and stood outside the Finch house. Jem could hear them talking with his father, but he did not know what about. He was frightened because he thought a mob had come after Atticus. But these were friends who had come to warn Atticus that there might be trouble when they moved Tom into the county jail next evening. The next night Atticus took the car and drove away. Later Jem, Scout, and Dill got dressed and went into town. There they found Atticus sitting in front of the jail. They did not go near him, however. When they saw some men get out of cars, Jem was again frightened and he and Scout ran to their father's side. Atticus was frightened for the children and tried to get them to go home, but they would not. A man grabbed Jem by the collar to send him home, but Scout kicked him. She spotted Walter Cunningham's father in the crowd and began chatting loudly about Walter and the Cunningham money troubles. Scout made Mr. Cunningham ashamed. He turned to the other men, and they all left together. Atticus was relieved, but he was also proud of his children because they had wanted to be with him when he was in trouble. The children were not at first aware that Mr. Underwood, editor of the Maycomb Tribune, had been watching the proceedings with a loaded double-barreled shotgun.

Comment

In this chapter the author describes contrasting scenes - the crowd outside the Finch house and the mob outside the jail. Jem is witness to both of these, and he is frightened in both cases. In the first scene, it is ignorance that makes him afraid. He cannot see who the men in the crowd are, nor can he hear what they are saying. His imagination runs wild with thoughts about the Ku Klux Klan and other lynch mobs that he has read about, but never seen. In the second case, it is the sight of real danger that makes him afraid. He sees the mob approach his father, and he knows what they want. Jem's reaction to fear in the first scene is to panic. He screams at his father that the phone is ringing. His reaction in the jail scene is to run to his father's side, and staunchly refuse to leave. Knowledge has given Jem a sense of control over the situation. He does not lose control of himself, or become blinded by emotion. The crowd is blinded by emotion and ignorance. But in their case, the ignorance is self-imposed, not simply lack of knowledge of the facts. Scout shames them by her innocent guilelessness.

Notes

venue - the county in which a law trial is held

criteria - the standards by which any judgment can be made

inaudible - not able to be heard

hideous - ugly

entailment - a limit put on an inheritance so that it cannot be transferred to another person

CHAPTER 16

Monday, the day for Tom Robinson's trial finally arrived. Atticus told the children not to go downtown; so they had to wait until lunchtime for news. To Scout the day seemed just like a Saturday. The whole county appeared to be coming into Maycomb for the trial. Miss Maudie thought it was morbid, the way everyone acted as though it was a Roman carnival, but Jem told her that the trial had to be public. When Atticus came home for lunch, he told the children that the jury had been selected. After he returned to town, Jem, Scout, and Dill followed. They had to be careful that Atticus did not see them; so they waited until all the white folks had gone into the courthouse. But there wasn't even standing room left. Luckily they met Reverend Sykes who took them with him to the Negro balcony where they were able to find seats.

Comment

This chapter yields yet another series of contrasts. On the one hand, there is the ever present snob - Aunt Alexandra - who thinks of the Negro only as a servant. She cautions Atticus against discussing things in front of Calpurnia. She tolerates the presence of a Negro because it's convenient. On the other hand, there is Braxton Bragg Underwood, an intense, profane man, who "despises Negroes, won't have one near him." Yet he is the one who, with his shotgun, made the evening watch with Atticus. It might be argued that he was protecting Atticus, not Tom Robinson. But Atticus was guarding the Negro, and many townspeople were highly critical of them for defending Tom. Miss Lee reinforces this contrast with numerous other examples, illustrating two typical sides of the Southern dilemma. For example, there is the incident of Miss Maudie and the narrow-minded foot-washing Baptists who hate her garden as a sinful display of vanity. Yet she refuses to go to the trial because she thinks it is a spectacle. They are marching on to see "justice done." There is also Mr. Dolphus Raymond who lives with a Negro woman. In spite of local criticism, he does what he wants to do and what he feels is right. Finally, there is Atticus himself. He did not ask for this case, he was appointed to it. However, he does not use that as an excuse for not doing the best job he can. He intends to defend Tom Robinson no matter what anyone might say. The case has become a matter of conscience with him. The author's sympathies, revealed through Scout's naive eyes, obviously lie with Atticus and men like him, who have the courage to do what they consider morally right, even though distasteful.

CHAPTERS 17 AND 18

The trial began, Judge Taylor presiding. Mr. Gilmer, the solicitor, called two witnesses. The first, Sheriff Heck Tate, reported the routine facts of the case. Mr. Ewell had come to get him. The sheriff found the girl badly bruised. She identified Robinson as her attacker. He testifies that the bruises on Mayella Ewell are on the right side of her face. The second witness, Bob Ewell, tells his version of the rape. He relates how he came home and found Tom Robinson with his daughter. His attitude is surly, but Judge Taylor makes him answer all the questions. The most important part of his testimony occurs when Atticus tricks him into showing that he is left-handed. Jem is jubilant about this because he feels that his father now has a very good chance of winning the case, if he can prove that Mayella was beaten by her father.

Mayella's Story

When Mayella comes to the witness stand, she is very nervous. She is afraid of Atticus and of what he is going to ask her. Her story is that she had asked Tom Robinson to break up a chiffarobe for her. When she went into the house to get something, Tom followed her. She turned around, and he attacked her. After Atticus had her repeat her story very carefully, he asked Tom Robinson to stand up. As it turned out, Tom had only one good arm, his right. The left had been mangled in a cotton gin when he was a boy. It was obvious to everyone that for him to rape a strong country girl like Mayella would have been very difficult.

Comment In these two chapters, the author gives a vivid picture of the other side of the case. The Ewells, we discovered earlier in the story, were ignorant country folk. They did not go to school, and they were not clean. Bob Ewell was a surly man who spent his relief checks on liquor rather than on food. Mayella, as we see in Chapter 18, is a lonely, frightened girl. She has no friends of her own age, and little social life.

Ewells vs. Negroes: The contrast between these poor whites and the Negroes is immediately apparent. Even though the colored people were outcasts, they had self-respect. Calpurnia had learned to read, and she had taught Zeebo to read. The Negro church-goers were poor, but they contributed their dimes to help Helen Robinson. The question that arises in the mind of the reader is why Bob Ewell should be so anxious to accuse a Negro of raping his daughter. The implication is that he did it as a cover-up for the fact that he had himself beaten Mayella. Bob Ewell is a white man but he is not accepted by his own group. He is surly in court because he feels inferior to Atticus and to Judge Taylor. He is dirty and poor because he is too lazy to be anything else. He is, in fact, lower than the Negroes, and hates them more for it. The only way he can maintain his white superiority is by persecuting a Negro. Tom Robinson becomes the scapegoat in Ewell's battle for pseudo-self-respect, the only means Ewell has of achieving social equality with the other whites. For him, it will justify his squalid, unproductive life. Unfortunately for him, however, he met his match in Atticus Finch. Instead of emerging as a hero, Bob Ewell emerges as a fool. Atticus has proven publicly that the Ewells were lying about Tom Robinson.

Notes

scamper - to run hurriedly

turbulent - disturbing

corroborating - supporting

infinite - unlimited

exodus - general departure

CHAPTER 19

When Tom Robinson gets on the witness stand, he tells a very different story. He describes how Mayella had been asking him for help for several months. On the day of the alleged rape, Mayella had put her arms around him and kissed him. She tried to get him to kiss her, but he was too frightened to do anything but run when he got the chance. Mr. Gilmer, of course, tried to make Tom look like a liar. The vicious manner in which he did this caused Dill to burst into tears. Scout had to take him outside so that he would not disturb the whole courtroom.

Comment

This chapter paints a vivid picture of loneliness, and of the desperation to which it can drive a person. Mayella Ewell waited for months for a chance to get some true affection. But Tom Robinson's life hangs in the balance because of her. Being a Negro, he could not yield to Mayella without getting the blame for her actions. By the same token, he did not dare strike her or push her in order to get away. If he had done so, he still could have been accused of attacking a white woman. Finally, the fact that he did run away when Bob Ewell appeared made it possible for the Ewells to say anything they wanted about him. Because he was a Negro in a white community he could count on no safety whatsoever. The townspeople always rallied to the defense of a white person, no matter how despicable. The fact that Tom Robinson, a Negro, should help Mayella Ewell, a white girl, because he felt sorry for her, was ironic. Mr. Gilmer sneered at him for suggesting that this was what he had done.

Dill Vs. Scout

The contrasting reactions of Dill and Scout are revealed in this chapter. Dill is himself an outcast of a sort. The author does not tell us much about his life in Meridian, but we do know that Dill's real father is not dead. We also know that Dill had been shuffled from relative to relative. When his mother remarried, he still did not feel wanted; so he ran away. Thus, Dill could not bear the sight of another outcast, Tom, being mistreated. It made him sick and caused him to weep. On the other hand, Scout had always been loved, had always had the security of a home. Her reaction is that, after all, this is Mr. Gilmer's job. Tom Robinson is just a Negro. True, she does realize that Mayella Ewell is probably the loneliest person in the world, and that Atticus is much kinder than Mr. Gilmer, but she is not particularly moved to pity by what she sees.

CHAPTER 20

Outside the courthouse, Scout and Dill met Mr. Dolphus Raymond. He gave Dill a sip from the bottle he carried in a paper sack. The townspeople had always thought that Mr. Dolphus had whiskey in that bottle, but it was really only Coca-Cola. Feeling better, Dill returned to the courtroom with Scout. Atticus was addressing the jury and pointing out that the prosecutor had proven nothing against Tom. In fact, the truth was obviously the opposite of what the Ewells claimed. Atticus ended his speech with a plea to the jury to believe him in the name of God.

Comment

We can compare the story of Mr. Dolphus with the speech made by Atticus Finch. Mr. Dolphus was, in a certain sense, lying to the townspeople. He created for their benefit the impression that he was drunk. In this way, although they disapproved of his life, they left him alone. They said he could not help himself. The same may be said of the case against Tom Robinson. The townspeople do not approve of the Ewells, but they are white. Because of this, they can be forgiven their way of life. The evidence is against the Negro because, just as nobody could see inside the paper sack where Mr. Dolphus hid his Coca-Cola, so nobody saw inside the Ewell cabin. Mr. Dolphus could pretend whiskey, and Bob Ewell could pretend rape. However, God created everybody with an equal right to justice. Therefore, Atticus pleads with the jury, in the name of God, to make a just decision to free the Negro.

Notes

detachment - aloofness

subsequent - following

integrity - honesty

circumstantial evidence - that which is not firsthand; there is no eyewitness to the crime

CHAPTERS 21 AND 22

When Calpurnia came to the courtroom, it was the first time that Atticus was aware that the children were present. He sent them home for supper. After eating, they returned to town to await the jury's decision. The obvious happens and Tom Robinson is convicted. As Atticus walked out, all the Negroes stood up, as a gesture of respect for him. The next morning the back porch is covered with gifts of food which the colored folks had sent. Atticus is so overcome with emotion that he cannot eat. Later, downtown, Bob Ewell spit in his face and swore to get him. Although he had lost the case, Atticus had proven that Bob Ewell was a liar.

Comment

In these two chapters we see the reaction of the characters to the trial. That Tom Robinson would be found guilty was a foregone conclusion. That Jem would weep because of it was not. He had been so certain that Atticus would win the case that the verdict of guilty caused tears of indignation. His own moral rectitude and innocence had made him believe that everyone must see the truth and have the courage to do right. He learned that night that adults sometimes have integrity only when it is expedient. When Miss Maudie cut him a piece from the large cake, it was a sign that he had taken a giant step toward manhood.

Dill's Reaction

On the other hand, Dill's reaction is perhaps more to be expected. He had already seen much of the adult world and had suffered personally from it. That he should become cynical is not surprising. He had given up the hope of expecting adults to be rational. His desire to become a clown and to laugh at the ways of adults is an example of this cynicism.

Maudie Vs. Stephanie

Miss Maudie and Miss Stephanie give us the contrasting views of the townspeople. Miss Maudie is their conscience, realizes, for she sees the right and realizes that Atticus stands for it. Miss Stephanie represents their self-righteousness. She is blinded to justice, and spends her mental energy being shocked by such things as the children sitting in the Negro balcony. Bob Ewell represents the bitterness of the townspeople. Like them he pretends to be good, but malevolence lurks under the surface. When the cloak of false virtue was removed from him by Atticus Finch, he struck back in the only way he knew. He promised more malevolent violence.

Notes

relenting - becoming less strict

exhilarated - enlivened

cynical - sarcastic

quiver - shake, tremble

dictum - a formal statement of opinion

CHAPTER 23

There is very little action in this chapter. Because of Bob Ewell's threat to kill Atticus, the children are frightened. He calms them by telling them that Bob Ewell is all talk. There is a general discussion of the trial and of how Jem and Scout react to it.

Comment

Miss Lee re-emphasizes Atticus' rational judgment in the discussion he has with the children, He explains that Tom would have gone free had twelve boys like Jem been on the jury. Jem is reasonable, but at Tom's trial they saw what happens when something comes between a man and his reason. Atticus also tells them how despicable he thinks it is to take advantage of a Negro's ignorance. For the first time, the children find out that one member of the jury, a Cunningham, had originally fought for acquittal. Scout is thrilled and announces plans to get to know Walter better and invite him to dinner. Aunt Alexandra gets upset, calling him "trash." As the children review the events of the past few weeks and months, they try to understand adults and their behavior. Scout decides that all this talk about classes of people is nonsense. "There's just one kind of folks. Folks." Jem reflects that if they're all alike, why do they go out of their way to despise one another? He says, "I think I'm beginning to understand why Boo Radley's stayed shut up.... It's because he wants to stay inside."

CHAPTER 24

Late in August of that summer, Aunt Alexandra was having a missionary tea. Jem and Dill were off swimming. Scout was helping to entertain the ladies. The talk was about the pagan Mrunas. The ladies were sorry for these poor, far-off people who lived such a savage life. They had no sympathy, however, for Tom Robinson, his wife, and the other Negroes. Suddenly, Atticus came home and called Alexandra into the kitchen. Tom Robinson was dead. He had tried to escape from the prison farm, and the guards had shot him.

Comment

The **irony** of this chapter is quite obvious. The Mrunas were far away and posed no threat. It was quite all right for the missionary ladies to feel sorry for their uncivilized and un-Christian life. On the other hand, the Negroes were close by and most of them tried to lead Christian lives. Tom Robinson was in jail on an unjust charge. Even in the face of this contradiction, the ladies felt justified in viewing the Negroes as inferiors. They agreed that Atticus had been wrong in trying to defend one of them. Even Alexandra, who had previously opposed her brother, could see the evasion in this type of thinking.

Scout's Lesson

The character most affected by the missionary tea was Scout. She was in the world of adults - a world which often mystified her. But she did learn a lesson from her aunt. After Atticus left with Calpurnia to go to the Robinson cabin, Aunt Alexandra had to do the serving. Nevertheless, she did not allow her emotions to show. She would not appear before these other women as anything but a lady. Scout learned a lesson in bravery. She also learned that Aunt Alexandra knew how to handle herself in a difficult situation. In other words, Scout concluded that background did mean something. Aunt Alexandra was able to continue with the missionary tea because she had been trained in a certain tradition. One part of that tradition was that one never allows a personal problem or feeling to interfere with the courteous treatment of other people.

Notes

impertinence - rudeness

squalor - wretchedness

sulky - sullen, ill-humored

undelectable - not enjoyable

CHAPTER 25

Atticus had picked up Jem and Dill on the way to Tom's, so they were present when Helen Robinson learned of the death of her husband. She fainted and had to be carried into her house. The town reacted to the death in its usual manner - with indifference. This was just one more "nigger" who had "cut and run." Mr. Underwood wrote an editorial in his paper likening Tom's death to the "senseless slaughter of songbirds by hunters and children." Bob Ewell "said it made one down and about two more to go."

Comment

This chapter is a bitter comment on the people of Maycomb. There was little sorrow that a man had died needlessly. Even Mr. Underwood's editorial made little impression on these people. They would forgive him his attempt at being dramatic. No one would cancel either subscriptions or advertising because of it. Scout finally realized the significance of the whole situation. Once Mayella Ewell starting screaming, Tom Robinson was a dead man. She realized that "in the secret courts of men's hearts Atticus had no case." In these circumstances, no Negro had the slightest chance of winning. It was color that determined right and wrong, truth and falsehood, and Tom Robinson was unfortunately black.

CHAPTER 26

At school that fall, during a discussion of current events, Miss Gates mentioned how terrible it was that Hitler was persecuting the Jews. Yet, on the night of the trial, Scout had heard her say that it was about time that somebody had taught the Negroes a lesson. The little girl could not understand how her teacher could hate Hitler so much, and then turn around and persecute the Negroes at home.

Comment

Miss Lee relentlessly pursues the contradictions and evasions of the bigoted mind. Miss Gates is well educated, but this does not seem to have helped her to be reasonable. Jem is upset by what Scout tells him, but not because of Miss Gates. He is trying to put the whole trial incident out of his mind. His youthful idealism was outraged by the jury's decision. Now he wants to try to forget the entire affair.

CHAPTER 27

Although things were pretty quiet after the trial, three things happened in Maycomb which indirectly affected the Finches. First, Bob Ewell got and quickly lost a job with the WPA. He blamed Atticus for his being fired. Then, one Sunday night, Ewell tried to burglarize Judge Taylor's house. Ewell also started annoying Helen Robinson. Link Deas, who had given her a job, had to threaten Ewell with jail in order to make him stop.

Comment

The events of this chapter foreshadow the final action of the novel. Bob Ewell had threatened to get Atticus Finch. After the death of Tom Robinson, he had said that there was one down and two to go. He tried to get Judge Taylor by burglarizing his house. But the judge was at home, and the attempt was not successful. Then Ewell tried to get at Atticus by annoying Helen Robinson. Thus, the scene is now set for the final blow. It is Hallowe'en, and Scout and Jem must go out alone past the Radley place to the school.

CHAPTER 28

Walking by the two big oaks on the Radley place, Scout and Jem are frightened by Cecil Jacobs who jumps out at them. Later, at the school, Scout falls asleep and misses her cue to come out on stage. She is too embarrassed to let anyone see her. Jem agrees to wait until everyone has left before taking Scout home. Because Scout has her costume on, Jem must lead her toward home. On the way, they sense that someone is following them. Suddenly they are attacked. When Scout finally gets herself untangled, she sees a strange man carrying Jem across the street. Running home, she finds that her brother is hurt. When Sheriff Tate arrives, he finds Bob Ewell lying dead under the oak tree.

Comment

The author carefully builds the suspense on the night of Ewell's death. First the two children are frightened by Cecil Jacobs. They come home alone in the dark. The Radley house lurks in the background. A stranger comes to their rescue when they are attacked. Thus the **climax** of the story is reached. Bob Ewell had sworn to get Atticus Finch. He had tried and failed. Now he lies dead under the oak tree on the Radley place.

The Pageant

There is a certain significance in the pageant too. It had been written to commemorate the glories of Maycomb. The people were self-satisfied and complacent about the way they lived. The auditorium was bright and gaily decorated for the presentation. But outside there was darkness, and evil lurked nearby. This is what the people of Maycomb had ignored. They had done Bob Ewell's dirty work by disposing of Tom Robinson, but they had not paid the slightest attention to the evil Ewell himself. In a similar way they had a detached interest in the Mrunas and in Hitler's persecution of the Jews. These were safely far away, and they could simply ignore injustices at home. They were too self-satisfied to think that real evil could threaten them.

CHAPTERS 29, 30 AND 31

Heck Tate and Atticus discuss what had happened. At first, Atticus thinks that it was Jem who killed Bob Ewell. Of course, it was not. Boo Radley was the mysterious stranger, and it was he who had saved the children. After Doctor Reynolds told them that Jem was going to be all right, Scout walked Boo Radley home. Standing on his porch, she saw the town from a different angle. Finally, she realized that Atticus was right. You can't understand other people until you get into their skin for a minute.

Comment

The story ends as it should. Justice has finally been done. Scout's understanding of the adult world has grown. For example, Boo Radley had always been a mystery to her before. She never knew the reason why he did not come out of his house. Now she sees him in a different light. All the while the children thought that they were spying on him, he was watching them. In spite of what they tried to do to annoy him, he came to their aid when they needed him. Somehow they had become his children, and he had protected them. Boo Radley, the alleged haunt, has been the instrument of justice for a town too cowardly to face the truth.

Concluding Thought

In the first chapter, it was mentioned that the world of the children was limited by a few houses. Their view of life was also limited. As the story progressed, the children learned much from their experiences. In the last chapter, Scout stands on the Radley porch. From it the neighborhood looks different to her. This is Boo Radley's view of the world. Scout has learned the lesson of tolerance. Atticus had told her that there were many different viewpoints in the world, and that she should never judge anyone else's ideas until she had looked at them from his point of view.

TO KILL A MOCKINGBIRD

CHARACTER ANALYSES

JEAN LOUISE FINCH

This character is probably the most important one in the story for the reader, because we view the action through her eyes and get her opinions about what is happening. Very aptly she is nicknamed Scout. At the beginning of the story she is six years old, and at the end she is eight. Scout is a very unusual little girl for many reasons. First of all, she is a tomboy, but is not difficult for the reader to understand. After all, her mother is dead, she idolizes her father, and she has her older brother as her only playmate throughout most of the story. Secondly, Scout is above average in intelligence. The reader knows this because, when Scout starts to school, she already knows how to read and to write. However, there is no indication in the story about how well she can do either of these; only that she can. Thus we don't have to conclude that she is in the genius class. We know that she picked up the reading from constantly being with her father, and the writing from Calpurnia. Thirdly, Scout is perceptive. By this is meant that she notices what is going on around her, and she has a certain ability to observe it. For example, at the trial she realized that Mayella Ewell must be the loneliest person in the world, and she was moved to sympathy by that thought. Lastly, Scout has a temper which gets her into occasional trouble. She would rather fight first and ask questions later. This gives her a sense of equality with her brother as she says about their fight in Chapter 14.

The Woman And The Girl

In studying the character of Scout, the reader must be careful. Actually there are two characters who are in reality one person. There is the grown Jean Louise who is telling the story, and there is the little girl Scout who is a part of the story. The reader should try to keep these two separate. The one is recalling what happened to her as a child. The other is the child herself going through the actions.

Atticus Finch

Atticus, Scout's father, is the central figure in the plot of the novel. The meaning of his name gives a clue to his character. Atticus is a term which refers to the ancient Greek city of Athens. It implies learning, culture, and heroism. Atticus Finch represents all of these things and more. To his children, he is a father whom they can love and respect, and to whom they can look for comfort and reasonable advice. To Tom Robinson and the other Negroes, he is a source of strength and of help. They respect him because they know he recognizes their personal dignity and that he will fight to protect it. To the townspeople, he is a symbol of integrity. Even though they criticize him for defending the Negro, they still re-elect him to the state legislature. Unconsciously, they know that they can count on him to do those things for them which they lack the courage to do for themselves.

Jeremy Finch

Jeremy is Scout's older brother. A boy of ten when the story opens, he is about thirteen when it ends. The events of the story parallel his transition from child to young man. His nickname, Jem, is appropriate. At the beginning of the story, he is a gem, a diamond in the rough that will be polished by the events in Maycomb. He emerges at the end of his experience completely changed by his contact with the adult world.

Of all the characters in the novel, Jem is the one who changes most during the course of the story. In the first chapters he is a rough and tumble boy, who accepts Dill's dare to run up to the Radley house. He tries to put the note through the shutter with the fishing pole. He sneaks into the Radley place at night in order to look into the window. As the story progresses, he becomes more sensitive to the meaning of the happenings around him. He develops a compassionate attitude toward Atticus, Tom, Boo Radley, and Mrs. Dubose because of a growing adult awareness of their problems. He has a more adult understanding of the Tom Robinson case than Scout and Dill. He wants his father to win it. In the courtroom, he listens attentively. However, when the jury convicts the Negro, he is shocked. His boyhood ideals of justice and honor have been shattered. He broods over man's ability to be so obviously unjust to his fellow man.

Charles Baker Harris

Charles Baker Harris is the character whom the reader might regard as the outside influence on the story. He is the only important character who is not from Maycomb. Like the other characters discussed so far, his name indicates his part in the story. Throughout the story he is referred to as Dill. The reader who is familiar with these matters knows that dill is a plant whose seeds are used to flavor other food; for example, the dill pickle. Thus Dill Harris is put into the story to flavor it. The reader does not know much about his background. The author tells us that he has been shuffled from relative to relative. Also, after his mother remarries, he does not feel that she really wants him. From the narrative the reader realizes that Dill is both imaginative and sensitive.

Dill's Place In The Novel

Dill has three important parts in this novel. First of all is that which concerns Boo Radley. Before Dill arrived on the scene, Jem and Scout merely wondered about the Radley place. They did not go near it. However, one of the first interests of Dill was to find out what was going on inside the house. It is he who dares Jem to act. If we say that the Radley house in this instance represents Maycomb, and the Radleys the townspeople who don't want their lives disturbed by anything unusual, then we can say that Dill represents the disturbing element. When we consider that he is an outcast of sorts, we might say that he represents the Tom Robinson case. This is the incident that disturbs the otherwise quiet town.

Secondly, Dill is a spectator at the trial. He is the outsider watching how Maycomb's system of justice works. What is the effect on him. It makes him sick, and then it makes him cynical. In this sense he represents another point of view. The people of Maycomb don't want their white-black society disturbed. But they cannot see it for the rotten thing that it is. They are too close to it. The outsider Dill, however, can see the gross injustice of it all, and he is disturbed by what he sees.

Thirdly, Dill is another in the story. He provides a companion for both Jem and Scout. As a boy, he can play boy's games with Jem. However, since he is closer in age to Scout than to the older Jem, he can share her problems better. He and Scout have a few talks together, such as the one on the night when he ran away from home.

Arthur Radley

Known to the children as Boo, Arthur appears only once in the story, at the end when he rescues Jem and Scout from Bob Ewell. Therefore, the reader does not know much about his personality except that he is a shy man, living in total seclusion. His real place in the story is as a symbol. He is a phantom that goes out only at night. In the beginning of the story, he is the symbol of the unknown. The children wonder about him and want to find out all they can about his life. At first they ask questions; later they invade the Radley property to satisfy their curiosity. Boo Radley becomes a symbol of kindness as he leaves various things in the tree for the children to find, and then covers Scout with a blanket on the night of Miss Maudie's fire. He becomes, in addition, a symbol of bravery. In the scene describing the Ewell attack on the children, Scout sees a strange man under the street light. He is walking as though carrying a burden too heavy for him. Even though a physically weaker man, Boo had no fear of the stronger Ewell. The **irony** of it all is that Boo Radley, the town freak, has a more genuine sense of values and greater compassion than most of the citizens of Maycomb. The children learn lessons of greater importance from Boo than they do from almost anyone else. They learn to judge him by his actions and not by town gossip.

Aunt Alexandra

Aunt Alexandra, Atticus' sister, represents the traditional values of the South - home, family, heredity, gentility, and white supremacy. She maintains all of these values even at the end of the novel. It is not she who changes, but Scout. Scout meets her aunt halfway. Aunt Alexandra represents the crucial problem of the South, then as now - an unwillingness to forsake a false value structure even in the face of evidence that it is meaningless and unjust.

Calpurnia

Calpurnia, the Finch family cook, is the link between the black and white worlds of Maycomb. She has a dual personality, acting in one way with her friends and in another with the Finches. She is practically accepted as a member of the Finch family. She treats the children as though they were her own. She does not spoil them; she helps Scout learn to write; she listens to their problems. Atticus is not afraid to talk openly in front of her because he knows that she understands. The author suggests that the Negro can be a valuable part of white society, if white men will only judge him on the basis of individual merit. Calpurnia's character also suggests a lesson for Negroes. They must learn to admire individual achievements, not as the aping of the white man's world, but as a necessity of dignified human life. Because both whites and blacks are guilty of racism, by not judging men individually, Cal must hide her achievements from both.

Miss Maudie Atkinson

Although this character does not play a great part in the story, she is perhaps one of the most colorful people in it. She is a benevolent, brave woman who loves floral beauty and the Finch children. Her bravery at the time of the fire foreshadows her valiant support of Atticus' defense of Tom. She is the most rational feminine character in the novel, one who repudiates Aunt Alexandra's value system.

Bob Ewell

Ewell represents the poor white trash of Maycomb. He is ignorant, irrational, slovenly, and totally unwilling to take any steps to improve himself. His hatred of the Negro is greater than anyone else's in Maycomb, because he knows he is inferior by any rational standard of comparison. He trades on the fact that Maycomb's standards are not rational, and that it will support his hunt for a scapegoat. He hopes to gain a self-respect he never earned by degrading Tom Robinson.

Mayella Ewell

Scout described Bob Ewell's daughter as the loneliest person in the world. In a sense she was the victim of circumstances. Her father's attitude prevented her from behaving like a normal person. Her desire for affection was genuine. Her lies were the result of fear of her father. In spite of what she does, the reader is sympathetic toward this poor girl who in some ways suffers more deeply than the Negroes of Maycomb.

Mrs. Henry Lafayette Dubose

This character is important only in relation to Scout and Jem. They learned a valuable lesson from her bravery in the face of impossible odds. They also learned that judgment of another human being requires that the context be known and evaluated.

Miss Stephanie Crawford

She represents the self-righteousness of the townspeople. Her stock in trade is vicious gossip aimed at almost anyone who offends her concepts of the status quo.

Judge Taylor

Judge Taylor is an elderly man well versed in the law. He seems to want to see justice done, but he is limited because the ultimate decision rests with the jury.

Tom Robinson

Tom's character is not well-drawn. He is a two-dimensional figure who seems to be a kind person. However, his ignorance and his position as a Negro cause his ultimate downfall.

Mr. Dolphus Raymond

He appears only briefly in the story, during the trial. Because he lives with a Negro woman, he is an outcast. But his children are the ones who suffer most because of this. Half black and half white, they belong to neither race and neither wants them. Both whites and blacks are guilty of intolerance.

Link Deas, Heck Tate, Mr. Underwood

These are minor characters who figure in the trial sequences. They are one segment of the white society in Maycomb, however, who seem to have a proper sense of justice.

Uncle Jack

He is Atticus's brother. Scout is very fond of him because he is kind and genial. He supports his brother's decision to defend Tom.

Uncle Jimmie

He is Aunt Alexandra's husband. He is an ineffectual husband and father, but Alexandra preserves the marriage at all costs to protect the family name.

Francis

Francis is Aunt Alexandra's grandson, who first gives the reader the family's reaction to the Tom Robinson case. He taunts Scout by calling Atticus a "nigger-lover."

The Cunninghams

They are a poor white family. They provide a contrast to the Ewells. They are industrious, proud, independent people who never accept anything that they cannot repay. One of the Cunninghams is almost responsible for a hung jury at the trial.

TO KILL A MOCKINGBIRD

COMMENTARY

SIGNIFICANCE OF THE TITLE

The Mockingbird

The title of this novel is first mentioned in Chapter 10. After Jem and Scout get air-rifles for Christmas, Atticus tells them to shoot all the blue jays they want, but that it is a sin to kill a mockingbird. Miss Maudie then explains that the mockingbird never harms anyone. All it does is sing. Therefore, it should be left alone. What is the significance of the symbol? Tom Robinson is an innocent person. He has never done anything to harm anyone. Actually, he had on many occasions helped Mayella Ewell because he felt sorry for her. Yet he is sentenced to death. After Tom is shot while trying to escape, Mr. Underwood compares him to a harmless songbird killed by senseless hunters. Boo Radley is also an innocent by-stander who is persecuted without reason.

Bird Imagery

Bird **imagery** highlights the significant events of the story. For example, when Atticus shoots the mad dog, the birds are not singing. On the night that Bob Ewell attacks the children, a lone mocker is singing in the Radley oak. Scout refers to Boo Radley himself as a mockingbird. After Heck Tate and Atticus decide that it is better to conceal the fact that Boo killed Bob Ewell, Scout says that to tell about this would be like killing a mockingbird. If people discovered what Boo had done, they would destroy the one thing he loved most - his privacy.

Who Killed Tom Robinson?

The mockingbird image can be interpreted in another way. A mockingbird is one that has no song of its own. It imitates the songs of other birds. The people of Maycomb are like this bird. Each conforms to the ways of the others, afraid to have identity, goals, or ideas separate from the group. Their way of life is an imitated routine passed from generation to generation. Atticus disturbs this routine, not content to leave well enough alone. One is reminded of the nursery **rhyme** that goes, "Who Killed Cock Robin?" The reader might ask himself the question: "Who killed Tom Robinson?" The answer in the nursery **rhyme** is: "I, said the sparrow/ With my little bow and arrow." The answer to our question is that the people of Maycomb, the mockingbirds who have no song of their own, are the ones who killed Tom Robinson. They let him be convicted and sent to prison on the basis of obvious lies. When he got tired of waiting for white man's justice and tried to run away, he was shot. Atticus tells the children that the people of Maycomb never served on juries for two reasons. First, they were not interested. Second, they were afraid that they might hurt someone's feelings if they had to pass a judgment involving two townspeople. In fact they feared the consequences of forsaking the safety of the group for the solitude of making an independent judgment.

BRIGHT NOTES STUDY GUIDE

THEME

Obvious Theme

The rather obvious **theme** of this book is the Negro question. The main plot of the story revolves around the Tom Robinson case. The significance of the title *To Kill A Mockingbird* applies directly to his death. Yet the reader cannot help but ask himself if this narrow message of racial equality is all that the author is trying to say. For instance, the book is full of remarks about seeing the other person's point of view. In Chapter 3, Atticus explains to Scout that she will get along better with people if she learns to climb into their skin once in a while, and try to see their point of view. The children are told to leave the Radleys alone because they were entitled to live in whatever way they so desired. Also one of Scout's difficulties throughout the story was that she could not understand some of Jem's ways. She had to be reminded frequently by Calpurnia and by Atticus to be patient with her older brother who was only going through a stage. She was still a little girl and he was emerging into manhood. Finally, the novel ends on the same note. After Scout returns from the Radley house, she sits by her father until she falls asleep. Her last words to him that night were that Boo was real nice. To this Atticus replied that most people were once you got to see them. The author uses the word "see" in this sentence, not the word "know." This carries out the idea of seeing the other person's viewpoint, not just knowing it.

Negro Point of View

The Negro problem can be tied in very nicely with the wider **theme** of trying to see the other person's point of view.

In Part I of the story, for example, Calpurnia seems to be taken pretty much for granted. Whatever she does, it is in her role of housekeeper, and there is very little comment made about her. Also in Part I of the story, there are two references made to Atticus defending Tom Robinson. In Chapter 9, Cecil Jacobs makes fun of Scout because her father defends Negroes. Later in this chapter, Francis refers to Atticus as a "nigger lover." In both instances Scout is ready to fight for her father's good name. But why? It's true that she did not understand Cecil's point of view, nor that of Francis. More important, though, is it that she did not understand the Negro's point of view. To her the names which Cecil and Francis called Atticus were offensive because she was a part of the same white society as these boys were. To have anything to do with Negroes was hateful, and she did not want her father connected with them.

However, in Chapter 12, Scout climbs into the skin of the Negro when she goes to Church with Calpurnia. There she sees first-hand the poverty of the Negro. Also she sees the ignorance of the Negroes who don't have hymn books because they cannot read them anyway. But, more importantly, she sees the openness of the Negro who allows his sins to be called out publicly. Then there is the generosity of the Negroes who, out of their poverty, give to help Helen Robinson. After this adventure, Scout has a little different viewpoint. She ceases to take Calpurnia for granted. She even wants to visit Calpurnia's home. Later, she is disturbed because Aunt Alexandra says that she cannot. Only once after this visit to the Negro church does Scout speak in any way unfavorably about the Negroes. That is in Chapter 19 when she is trying to console Dill. However, even this "after all, he's only a Negro." is rather an offhand attempt to make Dill feel better than a condemnation of the Negro himself.

Story of Experience

The **theme** of this novel may be extended even further than either the racial issue or the idea of trying to see the other person's point of view. For the three children, this is a story of experience. For Jem in particular, it is a story of initiation. At the beginning, he is an unsophisticated boy; but before the story is finished, he has learned much about the ways of adults. Thus we might say that the **theme** of this story is evil seen through the eyes of the innocent. The principal evil, of course, is that worked upon Tom Robinson. It is performed by the adults of Maycomb. The innocent are the three children, Jem, Scout, and Dill. As the story progresses, they learn more and more about the adult world until finally each child has his own reaction to it.

Adult Injustice

Although the primary evil is that worked upon Tom Robinson, this evil is foreshadowed by earlier events in the story. Probably the earliest example of this **foreshadowing** is Scout's first experience at school. Miss Caroline does not listen to her explanation about Walter Cunningham. Therefore, Scout is unhappy at school because she feels that the teacher punished her unjustly. However, it was not a desire to do the wrong thing, but Miss Caroline's ignorance of the people of Maycomb that led to this incident in the story. The second example of adult injustice is in Chapter 9. Uncle Jack spanks Scout because she used some bad words. However, he had not listened to her side of the story. Her feelings were hurt because Uncle Jack was someone she loved, and yet he had acted hastily in punishing her. Later, when Scout explains that she had socked Francis because of what he had said about her father, Uncle Jack is sorry. His mistake had been in not waiting to hear the whole story before he acted. The third example of adult injustice is in Chapter 11 when Mrs. Dubose verbally abuses the children. She uses them as something on which to take out her personal pain. Finally, she drives Jem into such a rage that he attempts to destroy her camellias. True, she tries to make up for this at the time of her death; but the injustice had been done. She had made Jem and Scout suffer because she herself was suffering.

Children's Reaction

There are many small examples of this adult injustice, but the three we have mentioned are sufficient. After these experiences, therefore, the children come face to face with the trial of Tom Robinson. Jem, Scout, and Dill are all present on that day, but none of them really understand what is going on. Jem, who had been so sure of victory, weeps at the verdict. Scout, still very much the little girl, merely watches her father very intently as he strides from the courtroom. Dill had already been made sick by the sight of what was going on. After the trial, Jem and Scout get over it, although this takes much explaining from Atticus and Miss Maudie. As for Dill, the author does not tell us. He drops out of the story after making his remark about being a clown and laughing at folks. Perhaps he is the one most hurt by this whole affair. The reader must wonder about whether or not he does grow up to be the cynic.

TECHNIQUE OF THE AUTHOR

Simplicity

Harper Lee's technique has the virtue of straightforward simplicity. She starts the story with an after-event, and then returns to the beginning to develop suspense to the **climax** and conclusion. Her description of Jem's arm and of his feeling about it arouses the reader's interest in how his arm got broken. The reader is also captivated by the charming narration of a little girl.

Foreshadowing

A further examination of the book finds the technique a little more complicated. The reader discovers that the book is divided into two parts, and that the main plot does not occur until Part II. Part I tells a preliminary story. It introduces all the principal characters at the same time that it gives a background picture of Maycomb and its residents. Most importantly, Part I shows the reader the Finch family against the background of this Southern community. The first part is composed of eleven chapters, each of which introduces a character or a part of the **theme**, or foreshadows an event or idea that is fully described in Part II. For example, Chapter 9 introduces the story of Tom Robinson and foreshadows the **theme** of bigotry and injustice. Chapter 10 describes the shooting of the mad dog and demonstrates Atticus' courage, which will be sorely tried in Part II. Part I ends with Chapter 11 and the story of Mrs. Dubose's camellias. They are, in a sense, a symbol of the **theme** of the story. Camellias cannot be destroyed by simply breaking off their tops. They must be dug out by the roots. By the same token, the prejudice that exists in Maycomb cannot just be rubbed off at the surface. Its roots are deeply ingrained in the minds and hearts of the people.

Comparison and Contrast

If the reader examines the structure of the story even more closely, he will discover that the author uses another technique - that of dividing the chapters themselves loosely into parts. In many of the chapters the author compares or contrasts the ideas and actions of various characters. For example, in Chapter 12 there is a contrast between Calpurnia and Lulu. Chapter 16 compares Aunt Alexandra and Braxton Underwood. Then in Chapter 20, there is a comparison by action. The story of Mr. Dolphus compares with the speech of Atticus before the jury. The reactions of the children are compared throughout the entire novel.

Character Portrayal

Miss Lee's portrayals of children are outstanding. We understand their motivations quite thoroughly because we see them closely in dialogue with Scout. Jem is the most interesting, because in some ways he is the most complex character in the novel. Adult characterization suffers, however, because we can see adults only through a child's eyes. Scout's inability to understand them limits our ability to know the total context of their actions. We have to learn about them from other sources. Tom Robinson, for example, plays an important part in the plot, but he is a flat stick-figure who doesn't really live for us. In other cases, minor characters come to life primarily because of Scout's childish viewpoint of them.

LOCAL COLOR

Love of the South

Although the author is critical of some of the ways of the South, it is evident from the story that she loves her section of the country. She describes the people with a certain sympathy that can never be mistaken for hatred. Take, for example, the treatment of Bob Ewell. He is surly, mean, and vicious as a person. The Finches dislike his way of life and his actions, but even he is treated in a sympathetic manner. In Chapter 3, for instance, Atticus explains that it is better to ignore the actions of people like the Ewells rather than to try to make them do things against their will. At the end of the story, there is sadness for the death of a human being, even though it is one like Bob Ewell.

Local Color

The manner in which Miss Lee describes the South is referred to as local color. She tries to give it to the reader the way it really exists. She paints pictures of old houses and of worn-out buildings that give the impression of an old South. The dialogue she uses is that which captures the tone of southern speech. She spells words like "yawl" in the manner in which the southerner would pronounce "you all." Also the description of the Christmas dinner gives the reader the impression of the leisurely pace which is usually associated with the South.

Lee Vs. Other Authors

Some modern authors give a picture of the South that is quite different. William Faulkner, for example, most often shows it as a place that is decaying and rotten at its very roots. On the other hand, Miss Lee tries to show it as a place quite like the rest of the world. It is old, perhaps, and some of its traditions are worn out and faulty; but it is still beautiful. Its people, like people everywhere, have their own views on life. Although some of their ideas may be wrong, they still deserve to be able to express them.

TO KILL A MOCKINGBIRD

CRITICAL COMMENTARY

Having been published in 1960, *To Kill A Mockingbird* is a new novel. To pass a permanent judgment on it is very difficult. Like many other things, a novel cannot be fairly judged in its own times. The true test of its worth is its ability to last as a favorite among readers. Many novels which were outstanding successes at the time of their publication are now all but forgotten. Others which barely sold in their times are now regarded as classics. What the fate of *To Kill A Mockingbird* will be, no one can really say. Here we will take the remarks of a few critics and try to evaluate them.

Leo Ward, a critic for *The Commonweal*, had this to say in the December 9, 1960, issue:

"Both the style and the story seem simple, but no doubt it is quite an achievement to bring them to that happy condition. What a greenhorn from the North may enjoy most is how quietly and completely he is introduced to ways of seeing, feeling and acting in the Deep South."

George Bernard Shaw once said that an author had to take each sentence and work on it so that the finished product makes the reader think that the art of writing is simple. Mr. Ward thinks that both the style and the story are simple. In the section on technique, we pointed out that the style is not so simple as it appears at first glance. Harper Lee's keen use of **foreshadowing** and of comparison and contrast almost escape the notice of the reader. Yet they contribute greatly to the value of the book.

Don Uhrbrock, writer for the book review portion of *Life Magazine*, had this to say in the May 26, 1961, issue:

"... Miss Lee writes with a rare compassion that makes her novel soar. To me, it is the best contemporary novel I have read since 1939."

The critic here emphasizes the ability of the author to write with sympathy. His comparison is intended to be with John Steinbeck's *Grapes of Wrath*, a book which also has the ability to arouse compassion for a downtrodden people. For those people who think Steinbeck is a great novelist, this is rare praise for Miss Lee. However, other readers will find qualities in this book more to be admired than its ability to make us weep over social injustice. In our section on **theme**, we brought out the fact that the idea of this novel was more than just the need for social equality. Miss Lee presents the reader with a picture of evil as it is seen through the eyes of the innocent. The over-all **theme** of the book is understanding on all levels of society.

Frank H. Lyell, book review critic for the *New York Times Book Review*, had this to say about Miss Lee's style:

"The praise that Miss Lee deserves must be qualified somewhat by noting that oftentimes Scout's expository style has a processed, homogenized, impersonal flatness quite out of keeping with the narrator's gay, impulsive approach to life in youth. Also, some of the scenes suggest that Miss Lee is cocking at least one eye toward Hollywood. Moviegoing readers will be able to cast most of the roles very quickly, but it is not disparagement of Miss Lee's winning book to say that it could be the basis of an excellent movie."

The critic here is pointing out what is probably the main weakness of this novel. Miss Lee is trying to recapture the scenes of her youth. She has been very successful in telling a good story and in giving an accurate picture of the South. However, she sometimes allows herself to inject adult opinions into the mouth of a child. This is unavoidable if an author chooses to have a child narrate an adult book about adult problems. Though Scout is not always credible in expository narrative, her impulsive sense of life is very convincing in dialogue.

In the July 10, 1960, issue of the *New York Herald Tribune Book Review*, Harding Lemay stated of the story's themes:

"In her first novel, *To Kill A Mockingbird*, Miss Harper Lee makes a valiant attempt to combine two dominant **themes** of contemporary Southern fiction - the recollection of childhood among village eccentrics and the spirit-corroding shame of the civilized white Southerner in the treatment of the Negro. If her attempt fails to produce a novel of stature, or even of original insight, it does provide an exercise in easy, graceful writing and some genuinely moving and mildly humorous excursions into the transient world of childhood.

The two **themes** Miss Lee interweaves throughout the novel emerge as enemies of each other. The charm and wistful humor of the childhood recollections do not foreshadow the deeper, harsher note which pervades the later pages of the book. The Negro, the poor white girl who victimizes him, and the wretched community spirit that defeats him, never rise in definition to match the eccentric, vagrant, and appealing characters with which the story opens. The two worlds remain solitary in spite of Miss Lee's grace of writing and honorable decency of intent."

Mr. Lemay seems to admire the easy, graceful style of the author. However, his criticism that the two **themes** emerge as enemies of each other does not appear correct in the light of the author's use of comparison and contrast, as discussed in the section on technique. It seems fair to conclude that perhaps the author did not want the charm of childhood recollections to foreshadow the deeper, harsher notes of the later pages. Perhaps she intended them to contrast in order to better illustrate her **theme** of evil seen through the eyes of the innocent.

TO KILL A MOCKINGBIRD

ESSAY QUESTIONS AND ANSWERS

....

Question: Explain the historical background of the story.

Answer: *To kill A Mockingbird* takes place in the early 1930s. This is the time of the Great Depression in the United States. It is also a period of great social change, a time which has a great influence on the plot itself. For example, farmers, like the Cunninghams, were hurt by the depression. They depended solely upon their crops to make a living. When they could not sell their crops, the farmers became very poor. The crops rotted and there was little money to buy new seed. The only choice the farmers had was to leave their land and go to the city to find work. This was something that the Cunninghams, for example, did not want to do. Also, since Maycomb was a farm area and the town itself depended upon the farmers, the entire area was very poor.

The author makes reference to what is going on in Washington at the time. By this she means the social changes that the Roosevelt administration was making in the lives of the people of the United States. Things such as the NRA and the WPA were government designed to help restore economic growth. The implication is that the people of Maycomb needed to re-examine their way of life. Perhaps it was time that they broke with some of their rural traditions.

Question: Why can Atticus Finch be described as the central figure in the story?

Answer: Atticus Finch can be described as the central figure in the story because he embodies the **theme**. He fights for justice and tolerance. Throughout the story he is the one who advises the children to try to see the other person's point of view. He is the image of good with which the children contrast the evil they see around them. Atticus is also the chief protagonist of the plot. In some ways he represents the conscience of Maycomb, or whatever is left of it.

Question: Describe the background of the Finch family.

Answer: Simon Finch migrated from England to Philadelphia. He had been irritated at home by the persecution of the Methodists by the other Protestant sects. Eventually, Simon bought some slaves and settled on the banks of the Alabama River. There he established his homestead, Finch's Landing. For years it had been the custom of the men of the family to stay at the homestead and make their living from cotton. However, Atticus and his brother Jack broke with this tradition. The one left to practice law, the other to practice medicine. Alexandra, their sister, remained at Finch's Landing.

Question: Why was Aunt Alexandra so concerned about family and background?

Answer: Atticus had said that Alexandra was concerned about family and background because this was all she had left. There was not a dime of the family fortune remaining to his generation. This is a typical Southern reaction. Many people in the South, victims of "genteel poverty," cling to the past to give the illusion of security and position in the world. Aunt Alexandra had found neither of these with her husband, who was not interested in anything but his fishing. Atticus and Jack found new careers, new ways of life, and a new means to give them a sense of identity. Atticus found this in his law career, and in being both father and mother to his children. Jack Finch found it in medicine. But Alexandra had nothing but tradition.

Question: Explain some of the strengths and weaknesses of the novel.

Answer: Generally speaking, the novel is well-written. The action moves along at a good pace and does not get bogged down at any point. The **theme** of the novel is clear and well illustrated throughout the book. All of the major ideas are convincingly dramatized. The author never gets "preachy" but lets the reader judge for himself the morality of the issues. Perhaps the main weakness of the book lies in the character of Scout. Her reactions are not always as childlike as they should be. The author, who is telling the story in the first person, does not always capture a childish point of view. Occasionally, therefore, Scout appears too adult.

Question: Why is Dill a major character?

Answer: Dill is a major character because he represents an outside influence on the action of the story. When he arrives on the scene, his imagination and desire for adventure move the other children to try new things. For example, Dill's curiosity about the Radley place leads them to attempt to find out what Boo Radley looks like.

Since Dill is not a resident of Maycomb, he is not really a part of what is happening. He is only an observer. In other words, through him the author is giving a picture of what outsiders think of Southern "justice." When Dill cries and gets upset at the trial, he is a symbol of the outsider who gets disturbed when he sees what the Southerner is doing to the Negro.

Question: Explain the role of Jem in the story.

Answer: Jem reflects the mood of the story and of its **theme**. At the beginning of the story, when all is well, he is a happy child. As the story progresses, Jem grows into young manhood, going through a series of physical and mental changes. This represents the change of attitude that some modern Southerners are taking towards the Negro question. When the second part of the book takes up the story of Tom Robinson, Jem becomes moody and serious. At the trial he listens attentively. When the situation looks good for Tom, Jem is the one who shows confidence. Later, after Tom is convicted, Jem is the one who cries. Finally, when Bob Ewell attacks the children, Jem is the one who gets hurt. In fact, he will never fully recover from the effects of his broken arm. In other words, Jem represents the Southerner who does not approve of what his fellows are doing. However, just as he will always have the scars of his fight with Bob Ewell, so it seems he will never be able to escape the injustices of the Southern community.

Question: What type of novel is *To Kill A Mockingbird* and why?

Answer: *To Kill A Mockingbird* can be classified as a realistic novel because the author tries to faithfully record the situation just as it existed in the South at the time. She does not try to excuse the evil which she pictures in the book. There is no idealization - people are prejudiced and indifferent. However, she also shows that there are some reasonable people who do not sanction what is happening, and who try to do something about it.

Maycomb is a place that could very well exist since there are towns in the South exactly like it. The author has captured the speech of the Southerner, the climate, and the prevalent attitudes. She records, she does not pass first-hand judgment.

BIBLIOGRAPHY

Charles Moritz, editor, *Contemporary Biography Yearbook*. New York, 1961.

Don Uhrbrock, "Literary Laurels for a Novice," *Life Magazine*, May 26, 1961.

BOOK REVIEWS

Harding Lemay, *New York Herald Tribune Book Review*, July 10, 1960.

Frank H. Lyell, *New York Times Book Review*, July 10, 1960.

Leo R. Ward. *The Commonweal*, December 9, 1960.

CPSIA information can be obtained
at www.ICGtesting.com
Printed in the USA
BVHW082130131221
623925BV00013B/549